Design *by* Martin Storey

Styling *by* Sarah Hatton

Photography *by* India Hobson

Hair & make up *by* Michaela Taylor

Models *by* J'adore Melissa

Pattern checking *by* Kath Duckitt

Design Layout *by* Lyndsay Kaye

R O W A N Loves ...

creative focus™ worsted & pure wool superwash worsted

Here at Rowan we are really proud of our beautiful yarns and in this brochure series we aim to show these yarns some love.

The third in this series supports creative focus™ worsted & pure wool superwash worsted.

Featuring 9 designs, which can be knit in either yarn, giving you plenty of options for these transeasonal classics.

Several designs offer design options making the design your own.

We hope this brochure makes you fall in love with these two great yarns too.

astoria

cropped
option

using
Creative Focus™ Worsted
pattern page 42

driscoll
cropped
option

using
Pure Wool Superwash Worsted
pattern page 54

corona
sweater
option

---

using
Creative Focus™ Worsted
pattern page 50

driscoll

long
option

___

using
Creative Focus™ Worsted
pattern page 54

union

hat

---

using
Creative Focus™ Worsted

pattern page 53

bellerose

cardigan
option

_____

using
Creative Focus™ Worsted
pattern page 44

astoria

long
option

using
Pure Wool Superwash Worsted

pattern page 42

bellerose

sweater
option

---

using
Pure Wool Superwash Worsted
pattern page 44

bergen

cardigan

___

using
Creative Focus™ Worsted
pattern page 47

rockette

using
Pure Wool Superwash Worsted
pattern page 59

corona
cardigan
option

_____

using
Pure Wool Superwash Worsted
pattern page 50

skyland

shawl
option

_____

using
Pure Wool Superwash Worsted
pattern page 61

haven

sweater
option

---

using
Pure Wool Superwash Worsted
pattern page 56

skyland

scarf
option

---

using
Creative Focus™ Worsted
pattern page 61

haven

cardigan
option

_____

using
Creative Focus™ Worsted
pattern page 56

the yarns

Creative Focus™ Worsted
A lovely wool and alpaca blended worsted weight yarn

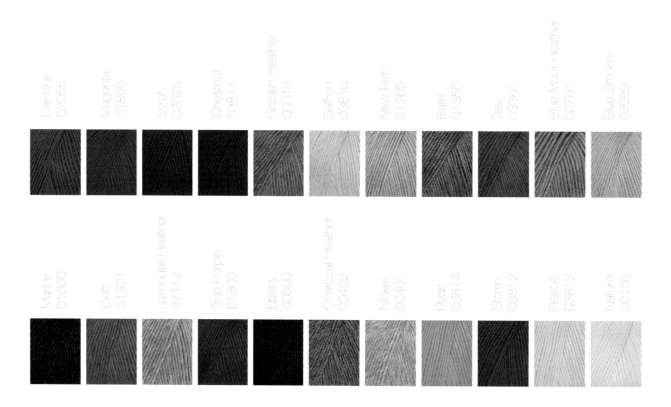

Pure Wool Superwash Worsted
A soft 100% Wool, machine washable worsted weight yarn, great all rounder with a stunning palette of shades

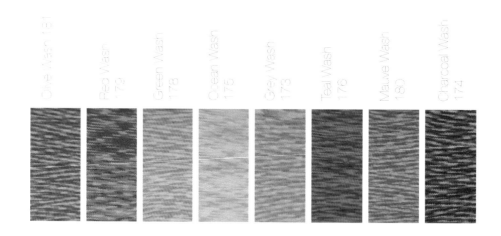

Mustard 131 Grasshopper 130 Apple 129 Olive 125 Jade 127 Bottle 140 Peacock 139 Garage 142 Lovat 161 Hawthorn 141 Hazel 126

Redcurrant 120 Raspberry 117 Rich Red 124 Cardinal 136 Papaya 135 Seville 134 Rust 106 Chestnut 107 Oak 159 Toffee 104 Gold 133 Buttercup 132

Pearl 162 Pretty Pink 113 Satin 116 Rose Pink 151 Candy 118 Splash 114 Vintage 158 Rosy 115 Magenta 119 Morello 121 Plum 122 Damson 150

Ivory 101 Soft Cream 102 Oats 152 Almond 103 Mole 157 Cocoa Bean 105 Clove 108 Moonstone 112 Granite 111 Charcoal Grey 155 Umber 110 Black 109

Oxygen 137 Azure 138 Aqua 156 Mallard 144 Electric 143 Navy 149 Oxford 148 Periwinkle 146 Breton 147 Ocean 145 Light Denim 154 Topaz 160 Light Navy 153

Astoria Sweater

main image page 21 & 4

To fit bust					
81-86	91-97	102-107	112-117	122-127	cm
32-34	36-38	40-42	44-46	48-50	in

Actual Bust					
108	118	130	142	156	cm
42½	46½	51¼	56	61½	in

Longer Sweater Length (at back neck)					
64	66	68	70	72	cm
25¼	26	26¾	27½	28¼	in

Shorter Sweater Length (at back neck)					
41	43	45	47	49	cm
16	17	17¾	18½	19¼	in

Sleeve Length					
45	46	47	47	47	cm
17¾	18	18½	18½	18½	in

YARN

For longer length sweater
Rowan Creative Focus™ Worsted

6	7	8	9	9	x 100gm

Or

Rowan Pure Wool Superwash Worsted

7	8	9	9	10	x 100gm

(shown in Hazel 128)

For shorter length sweater
Rowan Creative Focus™ Worsted

5	6	6	7	7	x 100gm

(shown in Natural 00100)
Or
Rowan Pure Wool Superwash Worsted

5	6	7	7	8	x 100gm

NEEDLES & NOTIONS
1 pair 4mm (UK 8 /US 6) knitting needles
1 pair 4.5mm (UK 7 /US 7) knitting needles
Stitch holders
Cable needle

TENSION
20 sts and 25 rows to 10cm/4in measured over pattern on 4.5mm (US 7) needles. Cable panel (30 sts) meas 10cm/4in.

PLEASE CHECK YOUR TENSION BEFORE COMMENCING, AND ADJUST NEEDLE SIZE IF NECESSARY

SPECIAL ABBREVIATIONS
C6B - slip next 3 sts onto a CN and holder at back of work, k3 then k3 from CN.
C6F – slip next 3 sts onto a CN and holder at front of work, k3, then k3 from CN.

BACK
Using 4mm (UK 8 /US 6) needles cast on
110 [118:130:142:158] sts.
Row 1 (RS): K2, * p2, k2, rep from * to end.
Row 2: * P2, k2, rep from * to last 2 sts, p2.
These 2 rows set rib.
Work in rib as set for 5 [5:6:6:6]cm, ending with WS facing for next row.
Next row (WS): Rib to end, dec 1 [0:0:0:1] st at each end of row. 108 [118:130:142:156] sts.
Change to 4.5mm (UK 7 /US 7) needles and cont as folls:-
For longer length version
Beg with a P row, cont in rev st st throughout until work meas 37 [38:39:40:41]cm/14½ [15:15½:15¾:16]in, ending with RS facing for next row.
For shorter length version
Beg with a P row, cont in st st throughout until work meas 14 [15:16:17:18]cm/ 5½ [6:6¼:6½:7]in, ending with RS facing for next row.
For both versions
Shape raglans
Cast off 5 [6:7:8:9] sts at beg of next 2 rows.
98 [106:116:126:138] sts.
Dec 1 st at each end of next 1 [5:11:19:27] rows, 1 [0:0:0:0] foll 4th row, then on every foll alt row to 42 [42:44:44:46] sts. **
Work 1 row, ending with RS facing for next row.
Leave rem sts on a holder.

FRONT

Using 4mm (UK 8 /US 6) needles cast on
146 [162:170:186:194] sts.
Row 1 (RS): K2, * p2, k2, rep from * to end.
Row 2: * P2, k2, rep from * to last 2 sts, p2.
These 2 rows set rib.
Work in rib as set for 5 [5:6:6:6]cm, ending with **WS** facing for next row.
For 2nd and 4th sizes only
Next row (WS): Rib2tog twice, rib to last 4 sts, rib2tog twice.
[158:182] sts.
For 1st, 3rd and 5th sizes only
Next row (WS): Rib to end, inc 2 [0:2] sts evenly across row.
148 [170:196] sts.
For all sizes
Change to 4.5mm (UK 7 /US 7) needles and cont as folls:-
Row 1 (RS): P5 [10:16:22:29], (k9, C6B, C6F, k9, p6) 3 times, k9, C6B, C6F, k9, purl to end.
Row 2 and foll alt rows: K5 [10:16:22:29], p30, (k6, p30) 3 times, knit to end.
Row 3: P5 [10:16:22:29], (k6, C6B, k6, C6F, k6, p6) 3 times, k6, C6B, k6, C6F, k6, purl to end.
Row 5: P5 [10:16:22:29], (k3, C6B, k12, C6F, k3, p6) 3 times, k3, C6B, k12, C6F, k3, purl to end.
Row 7: P5 [10:16:22:29], (C6B, k18, C6F, p6) 3 times, C6B, k18, C6F, purl to end.
Row 8: K5 [10:16:22:29], p30, (k6, p30) 3 times, knit to end.
These 8 rows set cable pattern and rev st st.
Cont as set until work matches back to start of raglan shaping, ending with RS facing for next row.
Shape raglans
Cast off 5 [6:7:8:9] sts at beg of next 2 rows.
138 [146:156:166:178] sts.
Dec 1 st at each end of next 1 [5:11:19:27] rows, 1 [0:0:0:0] foll 4th row, then on 24 [25:22:19:15] foll alt rows.
86 [86:90:90:94] sts.
Work 1 row, ending with RS facing for next row.
Shape front neck
Next row: P2tog, patt 5 [5:8:8:11], turn and leave rem sts on a holder. 6 [6:9:9:12] sts.
Work each side of neck separately.
Dec 1 st at neck edge of next 3 [3:5:5:7] rows and AT SAME TIME at raglan edge of 2nd and 0 [0:1:1:2] foll alt rows. 2 sts.
Leave rem sts on a safety pin.
With RS facing, leave centre 72 [72:70:70:68] sts on a holder, rejoin yarn to rem sts and patt to end.
Complete to match first side of neck, reversing all shapings.

SLEEVES (Both alike)

Using 4mm (UK 8 /US 6) needles cast on 46 [50:50:54:54] sts.
Work 12 rows in rib as set on Back, ending with RS facing for next row.
Change to 4.5mm (UK 7 /US 7) needles, beg with a P row, working in rev st st throughout cont as folls:-

Inc 1 st at each end of 3rd and 11 [2:7:13:22] foll 6th [4th:4th:4th:4th] rows, then on every foll 8th [6th:6th:6th:6th] row to 76 [84:88:96:102] sts.
Cont without shaping until sleeve meas 45 [46:47:47:47]cm / 17¾[18:18½ :18½:18½]in, ending with RS facing for next row.

Shape sleeve raglan
Cast off 5 [6:7:8:9] sts at beg of next 2 rows.
66 [72:74:80:84] sts.
Dec 1 st at each end of next 1 [1:1:3:5] rows, 3 [1:1:0:0] foll 4th rows, then on every foll alt rows to 14 sts.
Work 1 row, ending with RS facing for next row.
Leave rem sts on a holder.

MAKING UP

Using mattress stitch, join raglan seams, leaving left back raglan open.
Neckband
With RS facing, using 4mm (UK 8 /US 6) needles knit across 14 sts from sleeve holder, pick up and knit 4 [4:6:6:8] sts down left side of neck, knit across 72 [72:70:70:68] sts from holder for front neck as folls:- k0 [0:5:5:4], (k2tog, k1) 24 [24:20:20:20] times, k0 [0:5:5:4], pick up and knit 4 [4:6:6:8] sts up right side of neck, 14 sts from sleeve holder and 42 [42:44:44:46] sts from back neck holder. 126 [126:134:134:138] sts.
Beg with 2nd row, work in rib as set on back for 5cm/2in, ending with **WS** facing for next row.
Next row (WS): P7 [7:6:6:8], * p2tog, p8 [8:9:9:9], rep from * to last 9 [9:7:7:9] sts, p2tog, p7 [7:5:5:7].
114 [114:122:122:126] sts.
Beg with a K row, work 10 rows in st st.
Cast off.

Join left raglan and neckband seam, reversing seam for st st roll. Join side and sleeve seams.

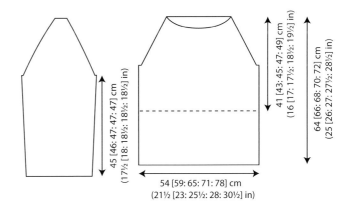

45 [46:47: 47: 47] cm
(17½ [18: 18½: 18½: 18½] in)

41 [43: 45: 47: 49] cm
(16 [17: 17½: 18½: 19½] in)

64 [66: 68: 70: 72] cm
(25 [26: 27: 27½: 28½] in)

54 [59: 65: 71: 78] cm
(21½ [23: 25½: 28: 30½] in)

Bellerose

main image page 24 & 18

To fit bust

81-86	91-97	102-107	112-117	122-127	cm
32-34	36-38	40-42	44-46	48-50	in

Actual Bust

88	98	110	122	136	cm
34¾	38½	43¼	48	53½	in

Length (at back neck)

57	59	61	63	65	cm
22½	23¼	24	24¾	25½	in

Sleeve Length

45	46	47	47	47	cm
17¾	18	18½	18½	18½	in

YARN
For sweater
Rowan Creative Focus™ Worsted

A 1	1	1	1	1	x 100gm
B 2	2	3	3	3	x 100gm
C 2	2	3	3	3	x 100gm
D 1	1	1	1	1	x 100gm

Or
Rowan Pure Wool Superwash Worsted
A Rose Pink 151

1	1	1	1	1	x 100gm

B Umber 110

2	2	3	3	3	x 100gm

C Oats 152

2	2	3	3	3	x 100gm

D Mustard 131

1	1	1	1	1	x100gm

For cardigan
Rowan Creative Focus™ Worsted
A New Fern 01265

1	1	1	1	1	x 100gm

B Charcoal Heather 00402

2	2	3	3	3	x 100gm

C Nickel 00401

2	2	3	3	3	x 100gm

D Golden Heather 00018

1	1	1	1	1	x100gm

Or
Rowan Pure Wool Superwash Worsted

A 1	1	1	1	1	x 100gm
B 2	2	3	3	3	x 100gm
C 2	2	3	3	3	x 100gm
D 1	1	1	1	1	x 100gm

NEEDLES & NOTIONS
1 pair 4mm (UK 8 /US 6) knitting needles
1 pair 4.5mm (UK 7 /US 7) knitting needles
Stitch holders

BUTTONS
6 buttons for cardigan

TENSION
20 sts and 25 rows to 10cm/4in measured over pattern on 4.5mm (US 7) needles.

PLEASE CHECK YOUR TENSION BEFORE COMMENCING, AND ADJUST NEEDLE SIZE IF NECESSARY

SWEATER
BACK
Using 4mm (UK 8 /US 6) needles and A cast on 86 [98:110:122:134] sts.
Row 1 (RS): K2, * p2, k2, rep from * to end.
Row 2: * P2, k2, rep from * to last 2 sts, p2.
These 2 rows set rib.
Work in rib as set for 8 [8:8:9:9]cm, ending with **WS** facing for next row.
Next row (WS): Rib to end, inc 2 [0:0:0:2] sts evenly across row. 88 [98:110:122:136] sts.
Change to 4.5mm (UK 7 /US 7) needles and cont as folls:-
Row 1: Using B, knit.
Row 2: Using B, purl.
Row 3: Using C, knit.
Row 4: Using C, purl.
These 4 rows set stripe sequence.
Working in stripe sequence as set throughout, cont as folls:-
Dec 1 st at each end of 1st [3rd:5th:5th:7th] row and 3 foll 4th rows. 80 [90:102:114:128] sts.

Work 11 rows without shaping, ending with RS facing for next row.
Inc 1 st at each end of next and 3 foll 6th rows.
88 [98:110:122:136] sts.
Cont in patt until work meas approx. 34 [35:36:37:38]cm/
13½ [13¾:14:14½:15]in, ending with row 4 [4:2:2:4] of stripe sequence and RS facing for next row.
Shape raglan
Cast off 5 [6:7:8:9] sts at beg of next 2 rows.
78 [86:96:106:118] sts.
For 1st size only
Row 1: K2, sl 1, k1, psso, knit to last 4 sts, k2tog, k2.
This row sets raglan shaping, dec 1 st as set as each end of 4th row. 74 sts.
Work 3 rows without shaping, ending with RS facing for next row.
For 2nd, 3rd, 4th and 5th sizes only
Row 1: K2, sl 1, k1, psso, knit to last 4 sts, k2tog, k2.
Row 2: P2, p2tog, purl to last 4 sts, p2togtbl, p2.
These 2 rows set raglan shaping, dec 1 st as set at each end of next [0:6:12:20] rows. [82:80:78:74] sts.
** **For all sizes**
Dec 1 st as set at each end of next and every foll alt row to 36 [36:38:38:40] sts.
Work 1 row, ending with RS facing for next row.
Leave rem sts on a holder.

FRONT
Work as given for Back to **.
For all sizes
Dec 1 st as set at each end of next and 16 [19:17:16:12] foll alt rows. 40 [43:44:44:48] sts.
Shape front neck
Next row (RS): K2, sl 1, k1, psso, k5 [8:8:8:11], turn and leave rem sts on a holder.
Work each side of neck separately.
Work 4 [6:6:6:8] rows, dec 1 st at neck edge of next 1 [3:3:3:5] row, then on 1 foll alt row and AT SAME TIME dec 1 st as set at raglan edge of next and every foll alt row. 4 sts.
Leave these 4 sts on a safety pin.
With RS facing, leave centre 22 [18:20:20:18] sts on a holder, rejoin yarn to rem sts and complete to match first side of neck reversing all shapings.

SLEEVES (Both alike)
Using 4mm (UK 8 /US 6) needles and D cast on
46 [50:50:54:54] sts.
Work 8cm in rib as set on back.
Change to 4.5mm (UK 7 /US 7) needles, beg with row 1 [3:3:3:1] of stripe sequence as set on back, inc 1 st at each end of 5th and – [-:8:8:6] foll – [-:6th:6th:4th] rows, then on every foll 10th [8th:8th:8th:6th] row to 64 [72:76:80:88] sts.
Cont without shaping until sleeve meas approx.
45 [46:47:47:47]cm/17¾ [18:18½:18½:18½]in, ending with row 4 [4:2:2:4] of stripe sequence and RS facing for next row.

Shape raglan
Cast off 5 [6:7:8:9] sts at beg of next 2 rows.
54 [60:62:64:70] sts.
Working raglan shaping as set on back, dec 1 st at each end of next and 4 [2:2:3:1] foll 4th rows, then on every foll alt row to 16 sts.
Work 1 row, ending with RS facing for next row.
Cast off rem sts.

MAKING UP
Join raglan seams, leaving left back raglan seam open.
Neckband
With RS facing, using 4mm (UK 8 /US 6) needles and A, pick up and knit 16 sts from left sleeve, 4 sts from safety pin at left front neck, 4 [6:6:6:8] sts down left side of neck, knit across 22 [18:20:20:18] sts from front neck holder, pick up and knit 4 [6:6:6:8] sts up right side of neck, 4 sts from safety pin at right front neck, 16 sts from right sleeve and 36 [36:38:38:40] sts from back neck holder. 106 [106:110:110:114] sts.
Beg with 2nd row, work 9 rows in rib as set on back.
Cast off in rib.

Join left back raglan and neckband seam. Join side and sleeve seams.

CARDIGAN
BACK
Work as given for Sweater.

LEFT FRONT
Using 4mm (UK 8 /US 6) needles and A cast on
43 [47:51:59:67] sts.
Row 1: * K2, p2, rep from * to last 3 sts, k2, p1.
Row 2: K1, p2, * k2, p2, rep from * to end.
These 2 rows set rib.
Work 8 [8:8:9:9] cm in rib, ending with **WS** facing for next row.
Next row: Rib to end, dec 2 [1:0:1:2] sts and inc 0 [0:1:0:0] st evenly across row. 41 [46:52:58:65] sts.
Change to 4.5mm (UK 7 /US 7) needles and work in stripe pattern as set until work meas approx. 34 [35:36:37:38]cm/
13½ [13¾:14:14½:15]in, ending with row 4 [4:2:2:4] of stripe sequence and RS facing for next row.
Shape raglan
Next row: Cast off 5 [6:7:8:9] sts, patt to end.
36 [40:45:50:56] sts.
Work 1 row.
For 1st size only
Row 1: K2, sl 1, k1, psso, knit to end.
This row sets raglan shaping, dec 1 st as set at beg of 4th row. 34 sts.
Work 3 rows without shaping, ending with RS facing for next row.
For 2nd, 3rd, 4th and 5th sizes only
Row 1: K2, sl 1, k1, psso, knit to end.

Row 2: Purl to last 4 sts, p2togtbl, p2.
These 2 rows set raglan shaping, dec 1 st as set at raglan edge of next [0:6:12:20] rows. [38:37:36:34] sts.
For all sizes
Dec 1 st as set at beg of next and 16 [19:17:16:12] foll alt rows. 17 [18:19:19:21] sts.
Shape front neck
Next row (WS): Cast off 8 [6:7:7:8] sts, patt to end.
9 [12:12:12:13] sts.
Work 4 [6:6:6:8] rows, dec 1 st at raglan edge as set on next and every foll alt row and AT SAME TIME dec 1 st at neck edge of next 3 [5:5:5:3] rows, then on 0 [0:0:0:2] foll alt rows. 4 sts. Leave these 4 sts on a safety pin.

RIGHT FRONT
Using 4mm (UK 8 /US 6) needles and A cast on
43 [47:51:59:67] sts.
Row 1: P1, k2, * p2, k2, rep from * to end.
Row 2: * P2, k2, rep from * to last 3 sts, p2, k1.
These 2 rows set rib.
Work 8 [8:8:9:9] cm in rib, ending with **WS** facing for next row.
Next row (WS): Rib to end, dec 2 [1:0:1:2] sts and inc 0 [0:1:0:0] st evenly across row. 41 [46:52:58:65] sts.
Change to 4.5mm (UK 7 /US 7) needles and work in stripe pattern as set until work meas approx. 34 [35:36:37:38]cm/ 13½ [13¾:14:14½:15]in, ending with row 1 [1:3:3:1] of stripe sequence and **WS** facing for next row.
Shape raglan
Next row: Cast off 5 [6:7:8:9] sts, patt to end.
36 [40:45:50:56] sts.
For 1st size only
Row 1: Knit to last 4 sts, k2tog, k2.
This row sets raglan shaping, dec 1 st as set at end of 4th row. 34 sts.
Work 3 rows without shaping, ending with RS facing for next row.
For 2nd, 3rd, 4th and 5th sizes only
Row 1: Knit to last 4 sts, k2tog, k2.
Row 2: P2, p2tog, purl to end.
These 2 rows set raglan shaping, dec 1 st as set at raglan edge of next [2:6:12:20] rows. [36:37:36:34] sts.
For all sizes
Dec 1 st as set at beg of next and 15 [18:16:15:11] foll alt rows. 18 [19:20:20:22] sts.
Work 1 row, ending with RS facing for next row.
Shape front neck
Next row (RS): Cast off 8 [6:7:7:8] sts, patt to last 4 sts, k2tog, k2. 9 [12:12:12:13] sts.
Work 1 row, ending with RS facing for next row.
Work 4 [6:6:6:8] rows, dec 1 st at raglan edge as set on next and every foll alt row and AT SAME TIME dec 1 st at neck edge of next 3 [5:5:5:3] rows, then on 0 [0:0:0:2] foll alt rows. 4 sts. Leave these 4 sts on a safety pin.

SLEEVES (Both alike)
Work as given for Sweater.

MAKING UP
Join raglan seams.
Neckband
With RS facing, using 4mm (UK 8 /US 6) needles and A, pick up and knit 14 [14:15:15:18] sts up right front neck, 4 sts from safety pin, 16 sts from right sleeve, 36 [36:38:38:40] sts from back neck holder, 16 sts from left sleeve, 4 sts from safety pin and 14 [14:15:15:18] sts down left front neck.
104 [104:108:108:116] sts.
Row 1 (WS): K1, * p2, k2, rep from * to last 3 sts, p2, k1.
Row 2: P1, k2, * p2, k2, rep from * to last st, p1.
These 2 rows set rib.
Work 7 rows more in rib as set.

Buttonhole band
With RS facing, using 4mm (UK 8 /US 6) needles and A, pick up and knit 120 [124:127:130:134] sts along right front and neckband edge.
Knit 3 rows.
Next row: K4 [4:5:4:4], cast off 2 sts, (k19 [20:20:21:22], cast off 2 sts) 5 times, knit to end.
Next row: Knit to end, casting on 2 sts by casting off sts on previous row.
Knit 3 rows.
Cast off knitwise on **WS.**

Button band
With RS facing, using 4mm (UK 8 /US 6) needles and A, pick up and knit 120 [124:127:130:134] sts along left front and neck-band edge.
Knit 8 rows.
Cast off knitwise on **WS.**

Join side and sleeve seams. Sew on buttons.

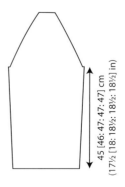
45 [46: 47: 47: 47] cm
(17½ [18: 18½: 18½: 18½] in)

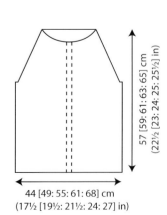
57 [59: 61: 63: 65] cm
(22½ [23: 24: 25: 25½] in)
44 [49: 55: 61: 68] cm
(17½ [19½: 21½: 24: 27] in)

Bergen

main image page 26 ◕ ◕

To fit bust

81-86	91-97	102-107	112-117	122-127	cm
32-34	36-38	40-42	44-46	48-50	in

Actual Bust

106	116	128	140	154	cm
41¾	45¾	50½	55¼	60¾	in

Length (at back neck)

64	66	68	70	72	cm
25¼	26	26¾	27½	28¼	in

Sleeve Length

45	46	47	47	47	cm
17¾	18	18½	18½	18½	in

YARN

Rowan Creative Focus™ Worsted

A Charcoal Heather 00402

4	4	4	4	4	x 100gm

B Nickel 00401

6	7	8	9	10	x 100gm

Or

Rowan Pure Wool Superwash Worsted

A 4	4	4	5	5	x 100gm
B 7	8	9	10	11	x 100gm

NEEDLES & NOTIONS

1 pair 4mm (UK 8 /US 6) knitting needles
1 pair 4.5mm (UK 7 /US 7) knitting needles
Stitch holders

TENSION

21 sts and 38 rows to 10cm/4in measured over pattern on
4.5mm (US 7) needles.

PLEASE CHECK YOUR TENSION BEFORE COMMENCING,
AND ADJUST NEEDLE SIZE IF NECESSARY

PATTERN NOTE

Due to the dense nature of this stitch we would recommend
when measuring your work you allow it to hang from the
needles rather than laying it flat.

BACK

Using 4mm (UK 8 /US 6) needles and A cast on
111 [121:135:147:161] sts.
Row 1 (RS): K1, * p1, k1, rep from * to end.
Row 2: * P1, k1, rep from * to last st, p1.
These 2 rows set rib.
Work 2 rows more in rib, ending with RS facing for next row.
Change to 4.5mm (UK 7 /US 7) needles and cont as folls:-
Row 1 (RS): Knit.
Row 2 and all other WS rows: P1, * k1 below, p1, rep from *
to end.
These 2 rows set patt.
Cont in patt until work meas 20cm/8in, ending with RS facing
for next row.
Change to B and cont in patt until work meas 40 [41:42:43:44]cm/
15¾ [16:16½:17:17¼]in, ending with RS facing for next row.

Shape raglans

Cast off 6 [6:8:8:10] sts at beg of next 2 rows.
99 [109:119:131:141] sts.
Next row: Patt 4, sl 1 knitwise, k2tog, psso, patt to last 7 sts,
k3tog, patt 4. 95 [105:115:127:137] sts.
This row sets raglan shaping.
Dec 2 sts as set at each end of 2 [6:10:17:21] foll 4th rows,
then on 11 [9:7:3:1] foll 6th rows. 43 [45:47:47:49] sts.
Work 1 row, ending with RS facing for next row.
Cast off rem sts in rib.

Pocket linings (Make 2)

Using 4.5mm (UK 7 /US 7) needles cast on 30 sts.
Beg with a K row, work in st st for 15cm, ending with **WS**
facing for next row.
Next row: Purl to end, inc 1 st at centre of row. 31 sts.
Leave these sts on a holder.

LEFT FRONT
Using 4mm (UK 8 /US 6) needles cast on 52 [58:64:66:74] sts.
Row 1 (RS): * K1, p1, rep from * to end.
Row 2: * K1, p1, rep from * to end.
These 2 rows set rib.
Work 2 rows more in rib.
Change to 4.5mm (UK 7 /US 7) needles and cont as folls:-
Row 1 (RS): Knit.
Row 2 and all other WS rows: K1, p1, * k1 below, p1, rep from * to end.
These 2 rows set patt.
Cont in patt until work meas 20cm/8in, ending with RS facing for next row.
Place pocket
Next row (RS): Using B, patt 10 [14:16:18:22], leave next 31 sts on a holder and in their place work across 31 sts from pocket lining holder, patt to end.
Using B throughout, cont in patt until work meas 40 [41:42:43:44]cm/ 15¾ [16:16½:17:17¼]in, ending with RS facing for next row.

Shape raglan and front neck
Next row: Cast off 6 [6:8:8:10] sts, patt to end.
46 [52:56:58:64] sts.
Work 1 row, ending with RS facing for next row.
Next row: Patt 4, sl 1 knitwise, k2tog, psso, patt to last 2 sts, patt 2tog. 43 [49:53:55:61] sts.
This row sets raglan shaping and front neck shaping.
Dec 2 sts as set at raglan edge of 2 [6:10:17:21] foll 4th rows, then on 11 [9:7:3:1] foll 6th row. and AT SAME TIME dec 1 st at neck edge of 6th [4th:4th:8th:6th] and 10 [2:13:6:2] foll 6th [4th:6th:8th:6th] rows, then on 1 [11:-:3:9] foll 8th [6th:-:10th:8th] rows. 5 sts.
Work 1 row, ending with RS facing for next row.
Leave rem sts on a safety pin.

RIGHT FRONT
Using 4mm (UK 8 /US 6) needles cast on 52 [58:64:66:74] sts.
Row 1 (RS): * P1, k1, rep from * to end.
Row 2: * P1, k1, rep from * to end.
These 2 rows set rib.
Work 2 rows more in rib.
Change to 4.5mm (UK 7 /US 7) needles and cont as folls:-
Row 1 (RS): Knit.
Row 2 and all other WS rows: * P1, k1 below, rep from * to last 2 sts, p1, k1.
These 2 rows set patt.
Cont in patt until work meas 20cm/8in, ending with RS facing for next row.
Place pocket
Next row (RS): Using B, patt 11 [13:17:17:21], leave next 31 sts on a holder and in their place work across 31 sts from pocket lining holder, patt to end.
Using B throughout, cont in patt until work meas 40 [41:42:43:44]cm/ 15¾ [16:16½:17:17¼]in, ending with **WS** facing for next row.

Shape raglan and front neck
Next row: Cast off 6 [6:8:8:10] sts, patt to end.
46 [52:56:58:64] sts.
Next row: Patt2 tog, patt to last 7 sts, k3tog, patt 4.
43 [49:53:55:61] sts.
This row sets raglan shaping and front neck shaping.
Dec 1 st at neck edge of 6th [4th:4th:8th:6th] and 10 [2:13:6:2] foll 6th [4th:6th:8th:6th] rows, then on 1 [11:-:3:9] foll 8th [6th:-:10th:8th] rows and AT SAME TIME dec 2 sts as set at each end of 2 [6:10:17:21] foll 4th rows, then on 11 [9:7:3:1] foll 6th row. 5 sts.
Work 1 row, ending with RS facing for next row.
Leave rem sts on a safety pin.

SLEEVES (Both alike)
Using 4mm (UK 8 /US 6) needles and A cast on 63 [63:67:67:71] sts.
Work 4 rows in rib as set on back.
Change to 4.5mm (UK 7 /US 7) needles and working in patt as set for Back, working inc sts into patt, inc 1 st at each end of 11th and 3 [4:3:6:7] foll 20th [12th:12th:10th:8th] rows.
71 [73:75:81:87] sts.
Work 1 [13:11:1:5] rows without shaping, ending with RS facing for next row.
Change to B and cont in patt, inc 1 st at each end of 19th [1st:3rd:9th:3rd] and 2 [-:-:7:2] foll 20th [-:-:10th:8th] rows, then on every foll 22nd [14th:14th:12th:10th] row to 79 [87:91:99:107] sts.
Cont without shaping until sleeve meas 45 [46:47:47:47]cm/ 17¾ [18:18½ :18½:18½]in, ending with RS facing for next row.

Shape raglan
Cast off 6 [6:8:8:10] sts at beg of next 2 rows.
67 [75:75:83:87] sts.
Working decreases as set on back, dec 2 sts at each end of next and 1 [3:1:5:6] foll 8th [4th:4th:4th:4th] row then on every foll 6th row to 15 sts.
Work 1 row, ending with RS facing for next row.
Cast off rem sts.

MAKING UP
Using mattress stitch, join all raglan seams.
Place a marker at centre of back neck.
Left front band
With RS facing, using 4mm (UK 8 /US 6) needles and B, starting at marker at centre back neck, pick up and knit 22 [22:22:22:23] sts from back neck, 15 sts from top of sleeve top, 5 sts from holder, 42 [42:46:46:49] sts down neck shaping and 91 [95:95:99:99] sts down front edge.
175 [179:183:187:191] sts.
Beg with 2nd row, work 15 rows in rib as set on back.
Cast off in rib.

Right front band
With RS facing, using 4mm (UK 8 /US 6) needles and B, pick up and knit 91 [95:95:99:99] sts up front edge, 42 [42:46:46:48] sts up neck shaping, 5 sts from holder, 15 sts from top of sleeve

top, 22 [22:22:22:23] sts from back neck ending at marker.
175 [179:183:187:191] sts.
Beg with 2nd row, work 15 rows in rib as set on back.

Pocket borders (Both alike)
With RS facing, using 4mm (UK 8 /US 6) needles and A,
working in rib as set on back across 31 sts left on a holder,
work 8 rows.
Cast off in rib.

Join front bands seam at back neck. Join side and sleeve
seams. Sew pocket borders and linings in position.

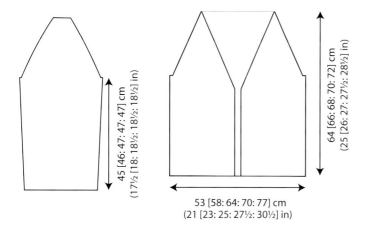

45 [46: 47: 47: 47] cm
(17½ [18: 18½: 18½: 18½] in)

64 [66: 68: 70: 72] cm
(25 [26: 27: 27½: 28½] in)

53 [58: 64: 70: 77] cm
(21 [23: 25: 27½: 30½] in)

Corona

To fit bust

81-86	91-97	102-107	112-117	122-127	cm
32-34	36-38	40-42	44-46	48-50	in

Actual Bust

109	119	131	143	157	cm
43	47	51½	56¼	62	in

Length (at back neck)

72	74	76	78	80	cm
28¼	29¼	30	30¾	31½	in

Sleeve Length

45	46	47	47	47	cm
17¾	18	18½	18½	18½	in

YARN

For sweater

Rowan Creative Focus™ Worsted

6	7	8	9	9	x 100gm

(shown in Basil 01350)

Or

Rowan Pure Wool Superwash Worsted

7	8	9	10	10	x 100gm

For cardigan

Rowan Creative Focus™ Worsted

6	7	8	9	9	x 100gm

Or

Rowan Pure Wool Superwash Worsted

7	8	9	10	10	x 100gm

(shown in Charcoal Grey 155)

NEEDLES & NOTIONS

1 pair 4mm (UK 8 /US 6) knitting needles
1 pair 4.5mm (UK 7 /US 7) knitting needles
Stitch holders

BUTTONS

5 buttons for cardigan

TENSION

20 sts and 25 rows to 10cm/4in measured over pattern on 4.5mm (US 7) needles.

PLEASE CHECK YOUR TENSION BEFORE COMMENCING, AND ADJUST NEEDLE SIZE IF NECESSARY

SWEATER
BACK

Using 4mm (UK 8 /US 6) needles cast on
110 [118:130:142:158] sts.
Row 1 (RS): K2, * p2, k2, rep from * to end.
Row 2: * P2, k2, rep from * to last 2 sts, p2.
These 2 rows set rib.
Work in rib as set for 8 [8:9:9:9]cm, ending with **WS** facing for next row.
Next row (WS): Rib to end, dec 1 [0:0:0:1] st and inc 0 [1:1:1:0] st at centre of row. 109 [119:131:143:157] sts
Change to 4.5mm (UK 7 /US 7) needles and cont as folls:-
Row 1: Knit.
Row 2 and all other WS rows: Purl.
Row 3: K2 [7:5:3:2] * yo, sl 1, k1, psso, k6, rep from * to last 3 [0:6:4:3] sts, (yo, sl 1, k1, psso) 1 [0:1:1:1] times, k1 [0:4:2:1].
Row 5: Knit.
Row 7: K6 [3:1:7:6], * yo, sl 1, k1, psso, k6, rep from * to last 7 [4:2:0:7] sts, (yo, sl1, k1, psso) 1 [1:1:0:1] times, k5 [2:0:0:5].
Row 8: Purl.
These 8 rows set pattern.
Cont in patt until work meas 38 [39:40:41:42]cm/ 15 [15½:15¾:16:16½]in, ending with RS facing for next row.
Work 28 rows more, ending with RS facing for next row.
Shape armhole
Dec 1 st at each end of next 5 [7:9:11:13] rows, then on 3 foll alt rows. 93 [99:107:115:125] sts. **
Cont without shaping until armhole meas 22 [23:24:25:26]cm/ 8¾ [9:9½:9¾:10¼]in, ending with RS facing for next row.
Shape shoulders and back neck
Next row (RS): Cast off 9 [10:11:13:13] sts, patt until there are 22 [24:26:28:32] sts on RH needle, turn and leave rem sts on a holder.
Next row: Cast off 2 sts, patt to end.
Next row: Cast off 9 [10:11:12:14] sts, patt to end.

Next row: Cast off 2 sts, patt to end.
Cast off rem 9 [10:11:12:14] sts.
With RS facing, working on rem sts, cast off 31 [31:33:33:35] sts, rejoin yarn to rem sts and patt to end.
Complete to match first side of neck, reversing all shapings.

FRONT
Work as given for back to **.
Cont without shaping until armhole meas 14 [15:15:15:16]cm/ 5½ [6:6:6:6¼]in, ending with RS facing for next row.
Shape front neck
Next row (RS): Patt 36 [39:43:47:52], turn and leave rem sts on a holder.
Work each side of neck separately.
Dec 1 st at neck edge of next 6 rows, 2 [2:3:3:4] foll alt rows, then on foll 4th row. 27 [30:33:37:41] sts.
Cont without shaping until armhole matches back to start of shoulder shaping, ending with RS facing for next row.
Shape shoulder
Next row: Cast off 9 [10:11:13:13] sts, patt to end.
Work 1 row.
Next row: Cast off 9 [10:11:12:14] sts, patt to end.
Work 1 row.
Cast off rem 9 [10:11:12:14] sts.
With RS facing, working on rem sts, leave 21 sts on stitch holder for neck, rejoin yarn to rem sts and patt to end.
Complete to match first side of neck, reversing all shapings.

SLEEVES (Both alike)
Using 4mm (UK 8 /US 6) needles cast on 46 [50:50:54:54] sts.
Work 8cm in rib as set on back, ending with **WS** facing for next row.
Next row (WS): Rib to end, dec 0 [1:0:1:0] st and inc 1 [0:1:0:1] st at centre of row. 47 [49:51:53:55] sts.
Change to 4.5mm (UK 7 /US 7) needles.
Row 1 (RS): Knit.
Row 2 and every foll WS row: Purl.
Row 3: Inc in 1st st, k2 [3:4:5:6], * yo, sl 1, k1, psso, k6, rep from * to last 4 [5:6:7:8] sts, yo, sl 1, k1, psso, k0 [1:2:3:4], inc in next st, k1. 49 [51:53:55:57] sts.
Row 5: (Inc 1 st in 1st st) 0 [0:0:1:1] time, knit to last 0 [0:0:2:2] sts, (inc in next st, k1) 0 [0:0:1:1] time. 49 [51:53:57:59] sts.
Row 7: (Inc 1 st in 1st st) 1 [1:1:0:1] time, k7 [0:1:4:4], * yo, sl 1, k1, psso, k6, rep from * to last 9 [2:3:5:6] sts, (yo, sl 1, k1, psso) 1 [0:0:1:1], k5 [0:1:3:2], (inc in next st, k1) 1 [1:1:0:1] time. 51 [53:55:57:61] sts.
Row 8: Purl.
These 8 rows set pattern and start sleeve shaping.
Working inc sts into patt where possible, inc 1 st as set at each end of 3rd [3rd:3rd:1st:1st] rows, 14 [13:-:-:2] foll 4th [4th:-:-:2nd] row, then on every foll 6th [6th:4th:4th:4th] row to 87 [89:95:99:103] sts.
Cont without shaping until sleeve meas 45 [46:47:47:47]cm/ 17¾ [18:18½:18½:18½]in, ending with RS facing for next row.

Shape sleeve top
Dec 1 st at each end of next 5 [7:9:11:13] rows, then on 3 foll alt rows. 71 [69:71:71:71] sts.
Work 1 row, ending with RS facing for next row.
Cast off 10 sts at beg of next 6 rows. 11 [9:11:11:11] sts.
Cast off rem sts.

MAKING UP
Using mattress stitch, join right shoulder seam.
Neckband
With RS facing, using 4mm (UK 8 /US 6) needles pick up and knit 20 [20:23:23:24] sts down left side of neck, knit across 21 sts on holder for front neck, pick up and knit 20 [20:23:23:24] sts up right side of neck, 3 sts down side of back neck, 31 [31:33:33:35] sts from back neck and pick up and knit 3 sts up side of back neck. 98 [98:106:106:110] sts.
Beg with 2nd row, work in rib as set on back for 9cm, ending with RS facing for next row.
Cast off in rib.

Join side and sleeve seams. Sew in sleeves using the semi set in method.

CARDIGAN
BACK
Work as given for back of Sweater.

Pocket linings (Make 2)
Using 4.5mm (UK 7 /US 7) needles cast on 30 sts.
Beg with a K row, work in st st for 15cm/6in, ending with RS facing for next row.
Leave these sts on a holder.

LEFT FRONT
Using 4mm (UK 8/US 6) needles cast on 51 [55:63:67:75] sts.
Row 1 (RS): * K2, p2, rep from * to last 3 sts, k2, p1.
Row 2: K1, p2, * k2, p2, rep from * to end.
These 2 rows set rib.
Work in rib as set for 8 [8:9:9:9]cm, ending with **WS** facing for next row.
Next row (WS): Rib to end, dec 0 [0:1:0:0] st and inc 0 [1:0:1:0] st at centre of row. 51 [56:62:68:75] sts.
Change to 4.5mm (UK 7 /US 7) needles and cont as folls:-
Row 1: Knit.
Row 2 and all other WS rows: Purl.
Row 3: K2 [7:5:3:2] * yo, sl 1, k1, psso, k6, rep from * to last st, k1.
Row 5: Knit.
Row 7: K6 [3:1:7:6], * yo, sl 1, k1, psso, k6, rep from * to last 5 sts, yo, sl 1, k1, psso, k3.
Row 8: Purl.
These 8 rows set pattern.
Cont in patt as set until work meas 18 [20:22:23:25]cm/ 7 [8:8¾:9:9¾]in from top of rib, ending with RS facing for next row.

Place pockets
Next row (RS): Patt 11 [13:16:19:23], slip next 30 sts onto a holder, patt across 30 sts from pocket holder, patt to end.
Cont in patt until work meas 38 [39:40:41:42]cm/ 15 [15½:15¾:16:16½]in, ending with RS facing for next row.
Shape front neck
Dec 1 st at neck edge (end) of next and 6 foll 4th rows.
44 [49:55:61:68] sts.
Work 3 rows, ending with RS facing for next row.
Shape armhole
Dec 1 st at armhole edge of next 5 [7:9:11:13] rows then on 3 foll alt rows and AT SAME TIME dec 1 st at neck edge of next and 2 [1:3:2:4] foll 4th rows, then on - [1:-:1:-] foll 6th row.
Dec 1 st at neck edge only of 4th row then on every foll 6th row to 27 [30:33:37:41] sts.
Cont without shaping until armhole matches back to start of shoulder shaping, ending with RS facing for next row.
Shape shoulder
Next row: Cast off 9 [10:11:13:13] sts, patt to end.
Work 1 row.
Next row: Cast off 9 [10:11:12:14] sts, patt to end.
Work 1 row.
Cast off rem 9 [10:11:12:14] sts.

RIGHT FRONT
Using 4mm (UK 8 /US 6) needles cast on 51 [55:63:67:75] sts.
Row 1 (RS): P1, k2, * p2, k2, rep from * to end.
Row 2: * P2, k2, rep from * to last 3 sts, p2, k1.
These 2 rows set rib.
Work in rib as set for 8 [8:9:9:9]cm, ending with **WS** facing for next row.
Next row (WS): Rib to end, dec 0 [0:1:0:0] st and inc 0 [1:0:1:0] st at centre of row. 51 [56:62:68:75] sts.
Change to 4.5mm (UK 7 /US 7) needles and cont as folls:-
Row 1: Knit.
Row 2 and all other WS rows: Purl.
Row 3: K8, * yo, sl 1, k1, psso, k6, rep from * to last 3 [0:6:4:3] sts, (yo, sl 1, k1, psso) 1 [0:1:1:1] times, k1 [0:4:2:1].
Row 5: Knit.
Row 7: K4, * yo, sl 1, k1, psso, k6, rep from * to last 7 [4:2:0:7] sts, (yo, sl1, k1, psso) 1 [1:1:0:1] times, k5 [2:0:0:5].
Row 8: Purl.
These 8 rows set pattern.
Cont in patt as set until work meas 18 [20:22:23:25]cm/ 7 [8:8¾:9:9¾]in from top of rib, ending with RS facing for next row.
Place pockets
Next row (RS): Patt 10 [13:16:19:22], slip next 30 sts onto a holder, patt across 30 sts from pocket holder, patt to end.
Cont in patt until work meas 38 [39:40:41:42]cm/ 15 [15½:15¾:16:16½]in, ending with RS facing for next row.
Shape front neck
Dec 1 st at neck edge (beg) of next and 6 foll 4th rows.
44 [49:55:61:68] sts.
Work 3 rows, ending with RS facing for next row.

Shape armhole
Complete to match left front, reversing all shapings.
SLEEVES (Both alike)
Work as given for sleeves of Sweater.

MAKING UP
Using mattress stitch, join both shoulder seams.
Place a marker at centre of back neck.

Buttonband
With RS facing, using 4mm (UK 8 /US 6) needles, starting at marker at centre back neck, pick up and knit 20 [20:21:21:22] sts from back neck, 74 [76:77:79:83] sts down left front neck and 88 [90:92:94:97] sts down left front edge to cast on edge.
182 [186:190:194:202] sts.
Beg with 2nd row, work 9 rows in rib as set on back.
Cast off in rib.

Buttonhole band
With RS facing, using 4mm (UK 8 /US 6) needles, starting at cast on edge, pick up and knit 88 [90:92:94:97] sts up right front edge to start of neck shaping, 74 [76:77:79:83] sts up neck edge and 20 [20:21:21:22] sts from back neck to marker.
182 [186:190:194:202] sts.
Beg with 2nd row, work 3 rows in rib as set on back.
Next row: Rib 4 [5:4:5:4], cast off 2 sts, (rib 17 [17:18:18:19], cast off 2 sts) 4 times, rib to end.
Next row: Rib to end, casting on 2 sts over gaps created by casting off sts on previous row.
Work 4 rows more in rib.
Cast off in rib.

Pocket borders (Both alike)
With RS facing, using 4mm (UK 8 /US 6) needles knit across 30 sts from holder.
Beg with 2nd row, work 9 rows in rib as set on back.
Cast off in rib.

Join buttonband seam at back neck. Join side and sleeve seams. Sew in sleeves using the semi set in method. Sew on buttons. Sew pocket borders and linings in position.

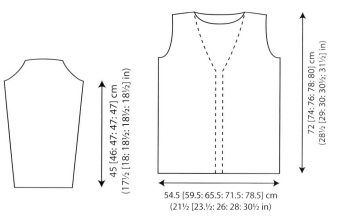

45 [46: 47: 47: 47] cm
(17½ [18: 18½: 18½: 18½] in)

72 [74: 76: 78: 80] cm
(28½ [29: 30: 30½: 31½] in)

54.5 [59.5: 65.5: 71.5: 78.5] cm
(21½ [23.½: 26: 28: 30½ in)

Union

main image page 16

SIZE
To fit an averaged size adult head

YARN
Rowan Creative Focus™ Worsted
1 x 100gm
(shown in New Fern (01265)
Or
Rowan Pure Wool Superwash Worsted
1 x 100gm

NEEDLES & NOTIONS
1 pair 4mm (UK 8 /US 6) needles

TENSION
19 sts and 37 rows to 10cm/4in measured over garter stitch
on 4mm needles.

PLEASE CHECK YOUR TENSION BEFORE COMMENCING,
AND ADJUST YOUR NEEDLE SIZE IF NECESSARY

Using 4mm (UK 8 /US 6) needles cast on 91 sts. (For a
neater finish we would recommend using the long tail/thumb
method.)
Working in garter stitch (every row knit) throughout cont until
work meas 17cm/6½in, ending with RS facing for next row.

Shape crown
Row 1 (RS): * K7, k2tog, rep from * to last st, k1. 81 sts.
Work 3 rows.
Row 5: * K6, k2tog, rep from * to last st, k1. 71 sts.
Work 3 rows.
Row 9: * K5, k2tog, rep from * to last st, k1. 61 sts.
Work 1 row.
Row 11: * K4, k2tog, rep from * to last st, k1. 51 sts.
Work 1 row.
Row 13: * K3, k2tog, rep from * to last st, k1. 41 sts.
Work 1 row.
Row 15: * K2, k2tog, rep from * to last st, k1. 31 sts.
Work 1 row.
Row 17: * K1, k2tog, rep from * to last st, k1. 21 sts.
Row 18: K2tog 10 times. k1. 11 sts.
Break off yarn and thread through rem sts. Fasten off.

MAKING UP
Join back seam. Make a pompon approx. 6cm/2¼in in
diameter and attach securely to top of hat.

Driscoll

main image page 8 & 13

To fit bust					
81-86	91-97	102-107	112-117	122-127	cm
32-34	36-38	40-42	44-46	48-50	in

Actual Bust					
111	121	133	145	159	cm
43¾	47½	52½	57	62½	in

Longer Sweater Length (at back neck)					
72	74	76	78	80	cm
28½	29	30	30½	31½	in

Shorter Sweater Length (at back neck)					
46	48	50	52	54	cm
18	19	19½	20½	21¼	in

Sleeve Length					
45	46	47	47	47	cm
17¾	18	18½	18½	18½	in

YARN
For longer length sweater
Rowan Creative Focus™ Worsted

7	7	8	9	9	x 100gm

(shown in Blue Heather 0791)
Or
Rowan Pure Wool Superwash Worsted

7	8	9	9	10	x 100gm

For shorter length sweater
Rowan Creative Focus™ Worsted

5	6	6	7	7	x 100gm

Or
Rowan Pure Wool Superwash Worsted

6	6	7	8	8	x 100gm

(shown in Gold 133)

NEEDLES & NOTIONS
1 pair 4mm (UK 8 /US 6) knitting needles
1 pair 4.5mm (UK 7 /US 7) knitting needles
Stitch holders

TENSION
20 sts and 25 rows to 10cm/4in measured over pattern on 4.5mm (US 7) needles.

PLEASE CHECK YOUR TENSION BEFORE COMMENCING, AND ADJUST NEEDLE SIZE IF NECESSARY

BACK
Using 4mm (UK 8 /US 6) needles cast on 111 [123:135:147:159] sts.
Row 1 (RS): K3, * p3, k3, rep from * to end.
Row 2: * P3, k3, rep from * to last 3 sts, p3.
These 2 rows set rib.
Work in rib as set for 5 [5:6:6:6]cm, ending with **WS** facing for next row.
Next row (WS): Rib to end, dec 0 [1:1:1:0] st at each end of row. 111 [121:133:145:159] sts. **
Change to 4.5mm (UK 7 /US 7) needles and cont as folls:-
For longer length version
Beg with a K row, cont in st st throughout until work meas 49 [50:51:52:53]cm/19 [19¾:20:20½:21]in, ending with RS facing for next row.
For shorter length version
Beg with a K row, cont in st st throughout until work meas 23 [24:25:26:27]cm/ 9 [9½:9¾:10¼:10¾]in, ending with RS facing for next row.
For both versions
Shape armhole
Row 1 (RS): K2, sl 1, k1, psso, knit to last 4 sts, k2tog, k2.
Row 2: P2, p2tog, purl to last 4 sts, p2togtbl, p2.
107 [117:129:141:155] sts.
These 2 rows set armhole shaping.
Dec 1 st at each end of next 3 [5:7:9:11] rows, then on 3 [3:2:2:2] foll alt rows. 95 [101:111:119:129] sts.
Cont without shaping until armhole meas 17 [18:19:20:21]cm/ 6½ [7:7½:8:8¼]in, ending with RS facing for next row.
Work 10 [10:12:12:14] rows more, ending with RS facing for next row.
Shape shoulders and back neck
Next row (RS): Cast off 9 [10:12:12:14] sts, knit until there are 24 [26:28:32:34] sts on RH needle, turn and leave rem sts on a holder.

Next row: Cast off 3 sts, purl to end.
Next row: Cast off 9 [10:11:13:14] sts, knit to end.
Next row: Cast off 3 sts, purl to end.
Cast off rem 9 [10:11:13:14] sts.
With RS facing, working on rem sts, leave 29 [29:31:31:33] sts on stitch holder for neck, rejoin yarn to rem sts and knit to end.
Complete to match first side, reversing shapings.

FRONT
Work as given for Back to **.
Change to 4.5mm (UK 7 /US 7) needles and cont as folls:-
Row 1 (RS): Knit.
Row 2: P39 [44:50:56:63], (k3, p3) 5 times, k3, purl to end.
These 2 rows set patt.
Cont in patt as set until work matches back to start of armhole shaping, ending with RS facing for next row.
Shape armhole
Working decs as set on Back, dec 1 st at each end of next 5 [7:9:11:13] rows, then on 3 [3:2:2:2] foll alt rows. 95 [101:111:119:129] sts.
Cont without shaping until armhole meas 17 [18:19:20:21]cm/ 6½ [7:7½:8:8¼]in, ending with RS facing for next row.
Shape front neck
Next row (RS): Patt 33 [36:41:45:50], turn and leave rem sts on a holder.
Work each side of neck separately.
Dec 1 st at neck edge of next 4 rows, then on 2 [2:3:3:4] foll alt rows. 27 [30:34:38:42] sts.
Work 1 row, ending with RS facing for next row. (Work should now match back to start of shoulder shaping).
Shape shoulder
Next row (RS): Cast off 9 [10:12:12:14] sts, patt to end.
Work 1 row.
Next row: Cast off 9 [10:11:13:14] sts, patt to end.
Work 1 row.
Cast off rem 9 [10:11:13:14] sts.
With RS facing, working on rem sts, leave 29 sts on stitch holder for neck, rejoin yarn to rem sts and patt to end.
Complete to match first side of neck, reversing all shapings.

SLEEVES (Both alike)
Using 4mm (UK 8 /US 6) needles cast on 46 [50:50:54:54] sts.
Row 1 (RS): K2, * p2, k2, rep from * to end.
Row 2: * P2, k2, rep from * to last 2 sts, p2.
These 2 rows set rib.
Work 10 rows more in rib, ending with RS facing for next row.
Change to 4.5mm (UK 7 /US 7) needles, beg with a K row, working in st st throughout cont as folls:-
Inc 1 st at each end of 3rd and 6 [5:10:7:13] foll 4th rows, then on every foll 6th row to 82 [86:90:92:96] sts.
Cont without shaping until sleeve meas 45 [46:47:47:47]cm/ 17¾[18:18½ :18½:18½]in, ending with RS facing for next row.
Shape sleeve top
Dec 1 st at each end of next 5 [7:9:11:13] rows, then on

3 [3:2:2:2] foll alt rows. 66 [66:68:66:66] sts.
Cast off 7 sts at beg of next 8 rows. 10 [10:12:10:10] sts.
Cast off rem sts.

MAKING UP
Using mattress stitch, join right shoulder seam.
Neckband
With RS facing, using 4mm (UK 8 /US 6) needles pick up and knit 14 [14:15:15:18] sts down left side of neck, knit across 29 sts on holder for front neck, pick up and knit 14 [14:15:15:18] sts up right side of neck, 6 sts down right side of back neck, knit across 29 [29:31:31:33] sts on holder for back neck and pick up and knit 6 sts up left side of back neck.
98 [98:102:102:110] sts.
Beg with 2nd row, work in rib as set on back for 9cm/3½in, ending with RS facing for next row.
Cast off in rib.

Join left shoulder and neckband seam. Join side and sleeve seams. Sew in sleeves using the semi set in method.

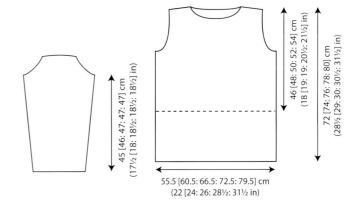

45 [46: 46: 47: 47] cm
(17½ [18: 18: 18½: 18½] in)

55.5 [60.5: 66.5: 72.5: 79.5] cm
(22 [24: 26: 28½: 31½ in)

46 [48: 50: 52: 54] cm
(18 [19: 19: 20½: 21½] in)

72 [74: 76: 78: 80] cm
(28½ [29: 30: 30½: 31½] in)

Haven

main image page 34 & 38

To fit bust					
81-86	91-97	102-107	112-117	122-127	cm
32-34	36-38	40-42	44-46	48-50	in

Actual Bust					
182	190	203	216	228	cm
71¾	75	80¼	85¼	90	in

Length (at back neck)					
56	58	60	62	64	cm
22	22¾	23¾	24½	25¼	in

Sleeve Length					
21	22	23	23	23	cm
8¼	8¾	9	9	9	in

YARN
For sweater
Rowan Creative Focus™ Worsted

8	9	9	10	11	x 100gm

Or

Rowan Pure Wool Superwash Worsted

9	10	11	11	12	x 100gm

(shown in Moonstone 112)

For jacket
Rowan Creative Focus™ Worsted

8	9	9	10	11	x 100gm

(shown in Blue Moor Heather 00791)
Or

Rowan Pure Wool Superwash Worsted

9	10	11	11	12	x 100gm

NEEDLES & NOTIONS
1 pair 4mm (UK 8 /US 6) knitting needles
1 pair 4.5mm (UK 7 /US 7) knitting needles
Stitch holders

BUTTONS
3 buttons for jacket

TENSION
19 sts and 33 rows to 10cm/4in measured over pattern on 4.5mm (US 7) needles.

PLEASE CHECK YOUR TENSION BEFORE COMMENCING, AND ADJUST NEEDLE SIZE IF NECESSARY

SWEATER
BACK
Using 4mm (UK 8 /US 6) needles cast on
197 [211:225:239:253] sts.
Row 1 (RS): K3, * p2, k5, rep from * to last 5 sts, p2, k3.
Row 2: P3, k2, * p5, k2, rep from * to last 3 sts, p3.
Row 3: K1, yo, sl 1, k1, psso, * p2, k2tog, yo, k1, yo, sl 1, k1, psso, rep from * to last 5 sts, p2, k2tog, yo, k1.
Row 4: As row 2.
These 4 rows set patt.
Work 27 rows more in patt, ending with **WS** facing for next row.
Next row (WS): Patt 6 [4:4:4:4], *patt 2tog, patt 6 [5:5:5:5], rep from * to last 7 [4:4:4:4] sts, patt2tog, patt 5 [2:2:2:2]. 173 [181:193:205:217] sts.
Change to 4.5mm (UK 7 /US 7) needles and cont as folls:-
Row 1: K1, * p1, k1, rep from * to end.
Row 2: * K1, p1, rep from * to last st, k1.
These 2 rows set moss stitch. **
Cont in moss stitch until work meas 48 [50:51:53:54]cm/
19 [19¾:20½:21½:21¼]in, ending with RS facing for next row.
Work 14 [14:16:16:18] rows, ending with RS facing for next row.
Shape shoulders
Cast off 9 [8:10:10:10] sts at beg of next 2 [6:4:10:6] rows.
155 [133:153:105:157] sts.
Cast off 8 [9:9:-:11] sts at beg of next 8 [4:6:-:4] rows.
Next row: Cast off 8 [9:9:10:11] sts, patt until there are 22 [24:24:26:28] sts on RH needle, turn and leave rem sts on a holder.
Work each side of neck separately.
Next row (WS): Cast off 3 sts, patt to end.
Next row: Cast off 8 [9:9:10:11] sts, patt to end.
Next row (WS): Cast off 3 sts, patt to end. 8 [9:9:10:11] sts.
Cast off rem sts.
With RS facing, working on rem sts, cast off 31 [31:33:33:35] sts, patt to end.

Complete to match first side of neck reversing all shapings.

FRONT
Work as given for Back to **.
Cont in moss stitch until work meas 48 [50:51:53:54]cm/
19 [19¾:20½:21½:21¼]in, ending with RS facing for next row.
Shape front neck
Next row (RS): Patt 76 [80:86:92:98], turn and leave rem sts
on a holder.
Work each side of neck separately.
Dec 1 st at neck edge of next 2 rows, then on 4 [4:5:5:6] foll
alt rows. 70 [74:79:85:90] sts.
Work 3 rows, ending with RS facing for next row. (Work
should now match back to start of shoulder shaping)
Shape shoulders
Working neck shaping as set on next and 4 foll 4th rows and
AT SAME TIME:-
Cast off 9 [8:10:10:10] sts at beg of next and 0 [2:1:6:2] foll alt
rows. 56 [45:54:10:55] sts.
Work 1 row, ending with RS facing for next row.
Cast off 8 [9:9:-:11] sts at beg of next and 5 [3:4:-:3] foll alt
rows. 8 [9:9:-:10] sts.
Work 1 row, ending with RS facing for next row.
Cast off rem sts.
With RS facing, working on rem sts, leave 21 sts on a holder,
patt to end.
Complete to match first side of neck, reversing all shapings.

SLEEVES (Both alike)
Using 4mm (UK 8 /US 6) needles cast on 50 [57:57:57:64] sts.
Work 31 rows in rib patt as set on back, working inc sts into
patt where possible, inc 1 st at each end of 11th and 3 [2:2:3:3]
foll 6th [8th:8th:6th:6th] rows. 58 [63:63:65:72] sts.
Next row (WS): P7 [6:6:7:7], * p2tog, patt 5, rep from * to last
9 [8:8:9:9] sts, p2tog, patt 7 [6:6:7:7]. 51 [55:55:57:63] sts.
Change to 4.5mm (UK 7 /US 7) needles and working in moss
stitch as set on back, inc 1 st at each end of 3rd and – [4:6:6:5]
foll – [8th:8th:6th:6th] row, then on every foll 6th [10th:10th:8th:8th]
row to 61 [65:69:71:75] sts.
Cont without shaping until work meas 21 [22:23:23:23]cm/
8¼ [8¾:9:9:9]in, ending with RS facing for next row.
Cast off 9 sts at beg of next 6 rows. 7 [11:13:17:21] sts.
Cast off rem sts.

MAKING UP
Using mattress stitch, join right shoulder seam.
Collar
With RS facing, using 4mm (UK 8 /US 6) needles pick up
and knit 24 [24:27:27:29] sts down left side of neck, 21 sts
from holder at front neck dec – [-:1:1:-] st at centre of these sts,
24 [24:27:27:29] sts up right side of neck, 6 sts down right
side of back neck, 31 [31:33:33:35] sts from back neck and
6 sts up left side of back neck. 112 [112:119:119:126] sts.
Row 1 (WS): K1, * p5, k2, rep from * to last 6 sts, p5, k1.
Row 2: P1, k5, * p2, k5, rep from * to last st, p1.

Row 3: As row 1.
Row 4: P1, k2tog, yo, k1, yo, sl 1, k1, psso, * p2, k2tog, yo,
k1, yo, sl 1, k1, psso, rep from * to last st, p1.
These 4 rows set patt.
Work 25 rows more in patt, ending with RS facing for next row.
Cast off in rib.

Using mattress stitch, join left shoulder and neckband seam.
Place markers 16 [17:18:19:20]cm/6¼ [6½:7:7½:8]in, down
from shoulder seams for armhole.
Join sleeve seams and sew in place between armhole
markers. Join side seams.

JACKET
BACK
Work as given for back of Sweater.

LEFT FRONT
Using 4mm (UK 8 /US 6) needles cast on 95 [95:102:109:116] sts.
Row 1 (RS): K3, * p2, k5, rep from * to last st, p1.
Row 2: K1, * p5, k2, rep from * to last 3 sts, p3.
Row 3: K1, yo, sl 1, k1, psso, * p2, k2tog, yo, k1, yo, sl 1, k1,
psso, rep from * to last st, p1.
Row 4: As row 2.
These 4 rows set patt.
Work 27 rows more in patt as set, ending with **WS** facing for
next row.
Next row: Patt 6 [6:10:5:8], * patt2tog, patt 8 [18:14:14:12],
rep from * to last 9 [9:12:8:10] sts, patt2tog, patt 7 [7:10:6:8].
86 [90:96:102:108] sts.
Change to 4.5mm (UK 7 /US 7) needles and cont as folls:-
Row 1 (RS): * K1, p1, rep from * to end.
Row 2: * K1, p1, rep from * to end.
These 2 rows set moss stitch.
Cont in moss stitch as set until work meas 22 [24:25:27:28]cm/
8¾ [9½:9¾:10¾:11]in, ending with RS facing for next row.
Shape front neck
Dec 1 st at neck edge (end) of next and 18 [18:19:19:20] foll
4th rows, then on every foll 6th row to 65 [69:74:80:85] sts.
Cont without shaping until left front matches back to start of
shoulder shaping, ending with RS facing for next row.
Shape shoulder
Cast off 9 [8:10:10:10] sts at beg of next and – [2:1:6:2] foll alt
rows. 56 [45:54:10:55] sts.
Work 1 row, ending with RS facing for next row.
Cast off 8 [9:9:-:11] sts at beg of next and 5 [3:4:-:3] foll alt rows.
Work 1 row, ending with RS facing for next row.
Cast off rem 8 [9:9:10:11] sts.

RIGHT FRONT
Using 4mm (UK 8 /US 6) needles cast on 95 [95:102:109:116] sts.
Row 1 (RS): P1, * k5, p2, rep from * to last 3 sts, k3.
Row 2: P3 * k2, p5, rep from * to last st, k1.
Row 3: P1, * k2tog, yo, k1, yo, sl 1, k1, psso, p2, rep from * to
last 3 sts, k2tog, yo, k1.

Row 4: As row 2.
These 4 rows set patt.
Work 27 rows more in patt as set, ending with **WS** facing for next row.
Next row: Patt 6 [6:10:5:8], * patt2tog, patt 8 [18:14:14:12], rep from * to last 9 [9:12:8:10] sts, patt2tog, patt 7 [7:10:6:8]. 86 [90:96:102:108] sts.
Change to 4.5mm (UK 7 /US 7) needles and cont as folls:-
Row 1 (RS): * K1, p1, rep from * to end.
Row 2: * K1, p1, rep from * to end.
These 2 rows set moss stitch.
Cont in moss stitch as set until work meas 22 [24:25:27:28]cm/ 8¾ [9½:9¾:10¾:11]in, ending with RS facing for next row.
Shape front neck
Dec 1 st at neck edge (beg) of next and 18 [18:19:19:20] foll 4th rows, then on every foll 6th row to 65 [69:74:80:85] sts.
Cont without shaping until right front matches back to start of shoulder shaping, ending with **WS** facing for next row.
Shape shoulder
Cast off 9 [8:10:10:10] sts at beg of next and – [2:1:6:2] foll alt rows. 56 [45:54:10:55] sts.
Work 1 row, ending with **WS** facing for next row.
Cast off 8 [9:9:-:11] sts at beg of next and 5 [3:4:-:3] foll alt rows.
Work 1 row, ending with **WS** facing for next row.
Cast off rem 8 [9:9:10:11] sts.

SLEEVES (Both alike)
Work as given for sleeves of Sweater.

MAKING UP
Join both shoulder seams.
Place markers 16 [17:18:19:20]cm/6¼ [6½:7:7½:8]in, down from shoulder seams for armhole.
Join sleeve seams and sew in place between armhole markers. Join side seams.
Place marker at centre back neck.

Buttonband and left collar
Using 4mm (UK 8 /US 6) needles cast on 11 sts.
Row 1 (RS): K2, * p1, k1, rep from * to last st, k1.
Row 2: K1, * p1, k1, rep from * to end.
These 2 rows set rib with g st edgings.
Cont as set until band, when slightly stretched, fits up left front edge from cast on edge to start of neck shaping, sewing in position at the same time and ending with RS facing for next row. **
Shape collar
Next row (RS): K1, increase in next st, rib to end.
This row sets increases.
Working inc sts into rib, inc 1 st as set every foll 6th row to 23 sts.
Cont without shaping until work is 1cm from marker at centre back neck, sewing in position at the same time, ending with RS facing for next row.
Next 2 rows: Patt to last 4 sts, wrap next st (by slipping next st

from left needle to right needle, taking yarn to opposite side of work between needles and then sliiping same stitch back onto left hand needle – when working back across wrapped sts, work the wrapped st and wrapping loop tog as one stitch) and turn, patt to end.
Next 2 rows: Patt to last 8 sts, wrap next st and turn, patt to end.
Next 2 rows: Patt to last 12 sts, wrap next st and turn, patt to end.
Next 2 rows: Patt to last 16 sts, wrap next st and turn, patt to end.
Work 2 rows.
Cast off in patt.

Mark positions for 3 buttons on this band, first to come 2.5cm up from lower edge and last to come just below neck shaping, with rem button evenly spaced between.
Buttonhole band and right collar
Using 4mm (UK 8 /US 6) needles cast on 11 sts.
Work as given for buttonband to **, and AT SAME TIME making buttonholes to correspond with positions marked as folls:-
Buttonhole row (RS): Rib 4, rib 2 tog, (yfwd) twice, sl 1, k1, psso, rib 3.
On following rows, work into front and back of double yfwd.
Shape collar
Next row (RS): Rib to last 2 sts, increase in next st, k1.
This row sets increases.
Working inc sts into rib, inc 1 st as set on every foll 6th row to 23 sts.
Cont without shaping until work is 1cm from marker at centre back neck, sewing in position at the same time, ending with **WS** facing for next row.
Next 2 rows: Patt to last 4 sts, wrap next st and turn, patt to end.
Next 2 rows: Patt to last 8 sts, wrap next st and turn, patt to end.
Next 2 rows: Patt to last 12 sts, wrap next st and turn, patt to end.
Next 2 rows: Patt to last 16 sts, wrap next st and turn, patt to end.
Work 1 row.
Cast off in patt.

Sew seam at back neck. Sew on buttons.

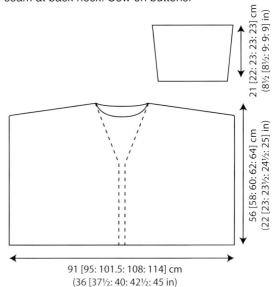

21 [22: 23: 23: 23] cm
(8½ [8½: 9: 9: 9] in)

56 [58: 60: 62: 64] cm
(22 [23: 23½: 24½: 25] in)

91 [95: 101.5: 108: 114] cm
(36 [37½: 40: 42½: 45] in)

Rockette

main image page 28

To fit bust					
81-86	91-97	102-107	112-117	122-127	cm
32-34	36-38	40-42	44-46	48-50	in
Actual Bust					
100	110	122	134	148	cm
39½	43¼	48	52¾	58¼	in
Length (at back neck)					
64	66	68	70	72	cm
25¼	26	26¾	27½	28¼	in
Sleeve Length					
45	46	47	47	47	cm
17¾	18	18½	18½	18½	in

YARN

Rowan Creative Focus™ Worsted

6 [6:7:7:8] x 100gm

Or

Rowan Pure Wool Superwash Worsted

6	7	8	8	9	x 100gm

(shown in Mallard 144)

NEEDLES & NOTIONS

1 pair 4mm (UK 8 /US 6) knitting needles

1 pair 4.5mm (UK 7 /US 7) knitting needles

Stitch holders

TENSION

20 sts and 25 rows to 10cm/4in measured over st st on 4.5mm (US 7) needles.

PLEASE CHECK YOUR TENSION BEFORE COMMENCING, AND ADJUST NEEDLE SIZE IF NECESSARY

BACK

Using 4mm (UK 8 /US 6) needles cast on 102 [110:122:134:150] sts.

Row 1 (RS): K2 * p2, k2, rep from * to end.

Row 2: * P2, k2, rep from * to last 2 sts, p2.

These 2 rows set rib.

Work in rib as set for 5 [5:6:6:6]cm, ending with **WS** facing for next row.

Next row (WS): Rib to end, dec 1 [0:0:0:1] st at each end of row. 100 [110:122:134:148] sts. **

Change to 4.5mm (UK 7 /US 7) needles and cont as folls:-

Beg with a K row, cont in st st throughout until work meas 43 [44:45:46:47]cm/ 17 [17¼:17¾:18:18½]in, ending with RS facing for next row.

Shape armholes

Cast off 8 [9:10:12:14] sts at beg of next 2 rows. 84 [92:102:110:120] sts.

Row 1 (RS): K2, sl 1, k1, psso, knit to last 4 sts, k2tog, k2.

Row 2: P2, p2tog, purl to last 4 sts, p2togtbl, p2. 80 [88:98:106:116] sts.

These 2 rows set armhole shaping.

Dec 1 st at each end of next 5 [7:9:9:11] rows, then on 1[1:1:2:1] foll alt rows. 68 [72:78:84:92] sts.

Cont without shaping until armhole meas 15 [16:16:17:18]cm/ 6 [6¼:6¼:6½:7]in, ending with RS facing for next row.

Work 12 [12:14:14:16] rows, ending with RS facing for next row.

Shape shoulders and back neck

Next row (RS): Cast off 8 [9:10:11:13] sts, knit until there are 12 [13:14:16:17] sts on RH needle, turn and leave rem sts on a holder.

Next row: Cast off 4 sts, purl to end. 8 [9:10:12:13] sts.

Cast off rem sts.

With RS facing, working on rem sts, leave 28 [28:30:30:32] sts on stitch holder for neck, rejoin yarn to rem sts and knit to end. Complete to match first side, reversing shapings.

FRONT

Work as given for Back to **.

Change to 4.5mm (UK 7 /US 7) needles, beg with a K row, working in st st throughout cont as folls:-

Work 2 [8:12:16:22] rows, ending with RS facing for next row.

Shape patch pocket

Next row: K84 [89:95:101:108], turn and leave rem sts on 1st holder.

Next row (WS): K2, p64, k2, turn and leave rem sts on 2nd holder.

Cont on these 68 sts only.

Next row: K2, sl 1, k1, psso, knit to last 4 sts, k2tog, k2. 66 sts.

These 2 rows set pocket shaping and garter stitch edging.

Dec 1 st as set at each end of 4th and 5 foll 6th rows, then on 3 foll 4th rows. 48 sts.

Work 1 row, ending with RS facing for next row.

Leave these sts on a 3rd holder.

Cast on 68 sts, then with RS facing, knit across 16 [21:27:33:40] sts from 1st holder. 84 [89:95:101:108] sts.

Next row: Purl to end, then purl across 16 [21:27:33:40] sts from 2nd holder. 100 [110:122:134:148] sts.

Cont on these sts for 48 rows more, ending with RS facing for next row. (Work should now match pocket in length)

Next row: K26 [31:37:43:49], (knit next st together with st from 3rd holder) 48 times, knit to end.

Beg with a P row, working in st st throughout, cont until front matches back to start of armhole shaping, ending with RS facing for next row.

Shape armholes

Cast off 8 [9:10:12:14] sts at beg of next 2 rows.

84 [92:102:110:120] sts.

Working dec as set on back, dec 1 st at each end of next 7 [9:11:11:13] rows, then on 1[1:1:2:1] foll alt rows.

68 [72:78:84:92] sts.

Cont without shaping until armhole meas 15 [16:16:17:18]cm/ 6 [6¼:6¼:6½:7]in, ending with RS facing for next row.

Shape front neck

Next row: K22 [24:27:30:34], turn and leave rem sts on a holder.

Work each side of neck separately.

Dec 1 st at neck edge of next 4 rows, then on 2 [2:3:3:4] foll alt rows. 16 [18:20:23:26] sts.

Work 3 rows without shaping, ending with RS facing for next row. (Work should now match back to start of shoulder shaping)

Shape shoulder

Next row: Cast off 8 [9:10:11:13] sts, knit to end.

8 [9:10:12:13] sts.

Work 1 row.

Cast off rem sts.

With RS facing, leave 24 sts on a holder, knit to end.

Complete to match first side of neck, reversing all shapings.

SLEEVES (Both alike)

Using 4mm (UK 6/US 6) needles cast on 46 [46:50:50:54] sts.

Work 5cm in rib as set on back, ending with RS facing for next row.

Change to 4.5mm (UK 7 /US 7) needles, beg with a K row and working in st st throughout, cont as folls:-

Inc 1 st at each end of 3rd and 7 [11:10:5:5] foll 8th [6th:6th:4th:4th]

rows, then on every foll 10th [8th:8th:6th:6th] row to 68 [76:80:86:90] sts.

Cont without shaping until sleeve meas 45 [46:47:47:47]cm/ 17¾ [18:18½ :18½:18½]in, ending with RS facing for next row.

Shape sleeve top

Cast off 8 [9:10:12:14] sts at beg of next 2 rows.

52 [58:60:62:62] sts.

Dec 1 st at each end of next 7 [9:9:9:7] rows, 4 [4:5:3:5] foll alt rows, 3 [3:3:5:5] foll 4th rows, 2 foll alt rows, then on 3 foll rows. 14 [16:16:18:18] sts.

Cast off 3 sts at beg of next 2 rows. 8 [10:10:12:12] sts.

Cast off rem sts.

MAKING UP

Using mattress stitch, join right shoulder seam.

Neckband

With RS facing, using 4mm (UK 8 /US 6) needles pick up and knit 11 [11:14:14:15] sts down left side of neck, knit across 24 sts on holder for front neck, pick up and knit 11 [11:14:14:15] sts up right side of neck, 4 sts down right side of back neck, knit across 28 [28:30:30:32] sts on holder for back neck and pick up and knit 4 sts up left side of back neck.

82 [82:90:90:94] sts.

Beg with 2nd row, work 9 rows in rib as set on back, ending with RS facing for next row.

Cast off in rib.

Join left shoulder and neckband seam. Join side and sleeve seams. Sew in sleeves using the semi set in method. Join seam at base of pouch pocket.

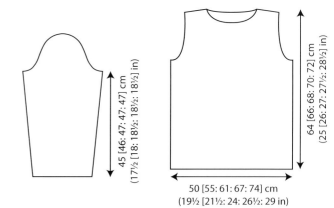

45 [46: 47: 47: 47] cm
(17¾ [18: 18½: 18½: 18½] in)

64 [66: 68: 70: 72] cm
(25 [26: 27: 27½: 28½] in)

50 [55: 61: 67: 74] cm
(19½ [21½: 24: 26½: 29 in)

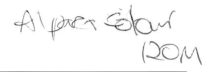

Alpaca Glow
120M

Skyland

main image page 32 & 36

Scarf
20cm(8in) at widest and 210cm (83in) in length

Shawl
42cm (16½in) at widest and 210cm (83in) in length

YARN
For scarf
Rowan Creative Focus™ Worsted
3 x 100gm (2 x 100gm if excluding pompons)
(shown in Magenta 01890)
Or
Rowan Pure Wool Superwash Worsted   200M
3 x 100gm

For shawl
Rowan Creative Focus™ Worsted
3 x 100gm
Or
Rowan Pure Wool Superwash Worsted
3 x 100gm
(shown in Mustard 131)

NEEDLES & NOTIONS
1 pair 4.5mm (UK 7 /US 7) knitting needles

TENSION
17 sts and 35 rows to 10cm/4in measured over garter stitch on
4.5mm (US 7) needles.

PLEASE CHECK YOUR TENSION BEFORE COMMENCING, AND
ADJUST NEEDLE SIZE IF NECESSARY

SCARF
Using 4.5mm (UK 7 /US 7) needles cast on 3 sts.
Row 1 (RS): Sl 1 knitways, knit into front and back of next st, k1.
Row 2: Sl 1 knitways, k1, knit into front and back of next st, k1. 5 sts.
Row 3: Sl 1 knitways, knit to end.
Row 4: Sl1 knitways, knit to end.
Rows 3 and 4 set garter st with slip st edges.
Row 5: Sl1 knitways, knit to end.
Row 6: Sl1 knitways, k1, knit into front and back of next st, knit to
end. 6 sts.
Rep rows 3 to 6, until there are 34 sts, ending with row 6 and RS
facing for next row.
Place marker at end of last row.

Working in garter st with slip st edges as set throughout cont until
work meas 142cm/56in from marker, ending with RS facing for next
row.
Cont as folls:-
Row 1 (RS): Sl 1 knitwise, knit to end.
Row 2: Sl 1 knitwise, knit to end.
Row 3: Sl 1 knitwise, knit to end.
Row 4: Sl 1 knitwise, k1, k2tog, knit to end. 33 sts.
Rep rows 1-4 until there are 3 sts, ending with row 4 and RS facing
for next row.
Next row: K3tog and fasten off.

MAKING UP
Make 2 pompons approx. 6cm/2½in in diameter and attach to
each end of scarf.

SHAWL
Using 4.5mm (UK 7 /US 7) needles cast on 5 sts.
Row 1 (RS): Sl 1 knitways, knit to end.
Row 2: Sl 1 knitways, knit to end.
Rep these 2 rows until work meas 30cm/12in, ending with RS facing
for next row.
Cont as folls:-
Row 1: Sl 1 knitways, knit to end.
Row 2: Sl 1 knitways, knit to end.
Row 3: Sl 1 knitways, knit to end.
Row 4: Sl 1 knitways, k1, knit into front and back of next st, knit to
end. 6 sts.
Rep rows 1 to 4 until there are 66 sts, ending with row 4 and RS
facing for next row.
Row 1 (RS): Sl 1 knitwise, knit to end.
Row 2: Sl 1 knitwise, knit to end.
Row 3: Sl 1 knitwise, knit to end.
Row 4: Sl 1 knitwise, k1, k2tog, knit to end. 65 sts.
Rep rows 1 to 4 until there are 5 sts, ending with row 4 and RS
facing for next row.
Place marker at end of last row.
Cont in garter sttich with slip stitch edgings until work meas 30cm
from marker.
Cast off.

MAKING UP
Make 2 pompons approx. 6cm/2½in in diameter and attach to
each end of scarf.

To help you enjoy a great knitting experience and a well fitting garment please refer to our sizing guide which conforms to standard clothing sizes. Dimensions in our sizing guide are body measurements, not garment dimensions, please refer to the size diagram for this measurment.

SIZING GUIDE

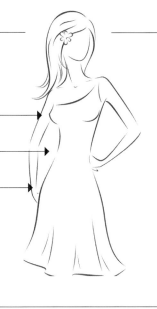

UK SIZE	S	M	L	XL	XXL	
DUAL SIZE	8/10	12/14	16/18	20/22	24/26	
To fit bust	32 – 34	36 – 38	40 – 42	44 – 46	48 – 50	inches
	81 – 86	91 - 97	102 – 107	112 – 117	122 – 127	cm
To fit waist	24 – 26	28 – 30	32 – 34	36 – 38	40 – 42	inches
	61 – 66	71 – 76	81 – 86	91 – 97	102 – 107	cm
To fit hips	34 – 36	38 – 40	42 – 44	46 – 48	50 – 52	inches

SIZING & SIZE DIAGRAM NOTE

The instructions are given for the smallest size. Where they vary, work the figures in brackets for the larger sizes. One set of figures refers to all sizes. Included with most patterns in this magazine is a 'size diagram' - see image on the right, of the finished garment and its dimensions. The measurement shown at the bottom of each 'size diagram' shows the garment width 2.5cm below the armhole shaping. To help you choose the size of garment to knit please refer to the sizing guide. Generally in the majority of designs the welt width (at the cast on edge of the garment) is the same width as the chest. However, some designs are 'A-Line' in shape or flared edge and in these cases welt width will be wider than the chest width.

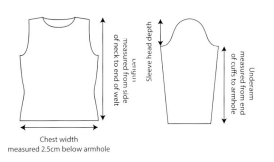

Chest width
measured 2.5cm below armhole

MEASURING GUIDE

For maximum comfort and to ensure the correct fit when choosing a size to knit, please follow the tips below when checking your size.
Measure yourself close to your body, over your underwear and don't pull the tape measure too tight!

Bust/chest – measure around the fullest part of the bust/chest and across the shoulder blades.

Waist – measure around the natural waistline, just above the hip bone.

Hips – measure around the fullest part of the bottom.

If you don't wish to measure yourself, note the size of a favourite jumper that you like the fit of. Our sizes are now comparable to the clothing sizes from the major high street retailers, so if your favourite jumper is a size Medium or size 12, then our Medium should be approximately the same fit.
To be extra sure, measure your favourite jumper and then compare these measurements with the Rowan size diagram given at the end of the individual instructions.
Finally, once you have decided which size is best for you, please ensure that you achieve the tension required for the design you wish to knit.
Remember if your tension is too loose, your garment will be bigger than the pattern size and you may use more yarn. If your tension is too tight, your garment could be smaller than the pattern size and you will have yarn left over.
Furthermore if your tension is incorrect, the handle of your fabric will be too stiff or floppy and will not fit properly. It really does make sense to check your tension before starting every project.

Tension

Obtaining the correct tension is perhaps the single factor which can make the difference between a successful garment and a disastrous one. It controls both the shape and size of an article, so any variation, however slight, can distort the finished garment. Different designers feature in our books and it is their tension, given at the start of each pattern, which you must match. We recommend that you knit a square in pattern and/or stocking stitch (depending on the pattern instructions) of perhaps 5 - 10 more stitches and 5 - 10 more rows than those given in the tension note. Mark out the central 10cm square with pins. If you have too many stitches to 10cm try again using thicker needles, if you have too few stitches to 10cm try again using finer needles. Once you have achieved the correct tension your garment will be knitted to the measurements indicated in the size diagram shown at the end of the pattern.

Chart Note

Many of the patterns in the book are worked from charts. Each square on a chart represents a stitch and each line of squares a row of knitting. Each colour used is given a different letter and these are shown in the materials section, or in the key alongside the chart of each pattern. When working from the charts, read odd rows (K) from right to left and even rows (P) from left to right, unless otherwise stated. When working lace from a chart it is important to note that all but the largest
size may have to alter the first and last few stitches in order not to lose or gain stitches over the row.

Working A Lace Pattern

When working a lace pattern it is important to remember that if you are unable to work both the increase and corresponding decrease and vica versa, the stitches should be worked in stocking stitch.

Knitting With Colour

There are two main methods of working colour into a knitted fabric: Intarsia and Fairisle techniques. The first method produces a single thickness of fabric and is usually used where a colour is only required in a particular area of a row and does not form a repeating pattern across the row, as in the fairisle technique.

Fairisle type knitting: When two or three colours are worked repeatedly across a row, strand the yarn not in use loosely behind the stitches being worked. If you are working with more than two colours, treat the "floating" yarns as if they were one yarn and always spread the stitches to their correct width to keep them elastic. It is advisable not to carry the stranded or "floating" yarns over more than three stitches at a time, but to weave them under and over the colour you are working. The "floating" yarns are therefore caught at the back of the work.

Intarsia: The simplest way to do this is to cut short lengths of yarn for each motif or block of colour used in a row. Then joining in the various colours at the appropriate point on the row, link one colour to the next by twisting them around each other where they meet on the wrong side to avoid gaps. All ends can then either be darned along the colour join lines, as each motif is completed or then can be "knitted-in" to the fabric of the knitting as each colour is worked into the pattern. This is done in much the same way as "weaving- in" yarns when working the Fairisle technique and does save time darning-in ends. It is essential that the tension is noted for intarsia as this may vary from the stocking stitch if both are used in the same pattern.

Finishing Instructions

After working for hours knitting a garment, it seems a great pity that many garments are spoiled because such little care is taken in the pressing and finishing process. Follow the text below for a truly professional-looking garment.

Pressing

Block out each piece of knitting and following the instructions on the ball band press the garment pieces, omitting the ribs. Tip: Take special care to press the edges, as this will make sewing up both easier and neater. If the ball band indicates that the fabric is not to be pressed, then covering the blocked out fabric with a damp white cotton cloth and leaving it to stand will have the desired effect. Darn in all ends neatly along the selvage edge or a colour join, as appropriate.

Stitching

When stitching the pieces together, remember to match areas of colour and texture very carefully where they meet. Use a seam stitch such as back stitch or mattress stitch for all main knitting seams and join all ribs and neckband with mattress stitch, unless otherwise stated.

Construction

Having completed the pattern instructions, join left shoulder and neckband seams as detailed above. Sew the top of the sleeve to the body of the garment using the method detailed in the pattern, referring to the appropriate guide:

Straight cast-off sleeves: Place centre of cast-off edge of sleeve to shoulder seam. Sew top of sleeve to body, using markers as guidelines where applicable.

Square set-in sleeves: Place centre of cast-off edge of sleeve to shoulder seam. Set sleeve head into armhole, the straight sides at top of sleeve to form a neat right-angle to cast-off sts at armhole on back and front.

Shallow set-in sleeves: Place centre of cast off edge of sleeve to shoulder seam. Match decreases at beg of armhole shaping to decreases at top of sleeve. Sew sleeve head into armhole, easing in shapings.

Set-in sleeves: Place centre of cast-off edge of sleeve to shoulder seam. Set in sleeve, easing sleeve head into armhole.

Join side and sleeve seams.

Slip stitch pocket edgings and linings into place.

Sew on buttons to correspond with buttonholes.

Ribbed welts and neckbands and any areas of garter stitch should not be pressed.

ABBREVIATIONS

K	knit
P	purl
st(s)	stitch(es)
inc	increas(e)(ing)
dec	decreas(e)(ing)
st st	stocking stitch (1 row K, 1 row P)
g st	garter stitch (K every row)
beg	begin(ning)
foll	following
rem	remain(ing)
rep	repeat
alt	alternate
cont	continue
patt	pattern
tog	together
mm	millimetres
cm	centimetres
in(s)	inch(es)
RS	right side
WS	wrong side
sl 1	slip one stitch
psso	pass slipped stitch over
tbl	through back of loop
rh	right hand
lh	left hand
wyif	with yarn in front
wyib	with yarn at back
yo	yarn over
skp	slip 1, knit 1,psso
m1l	pick up loop between last and next stitch from the front and knit into the back of this loop
m1r	pick up loop between last and next stitch from behind and work into the front of this loop
kfb	knit into front and back
yfwd	yarn forward
meas	measures
0	no stitches, times or rows
-	no stitches, times or rows for that size
yo	yarn over needle
sl2togK	slip 2 stitches together knitways

EXPERIENCE RATINGS
For guidance only

Easy, straight forward knitting

For the more experienced knitter

Advanced techniques used

WASHCARE SYMBOLS

machine wash

hand wash

dry clean

Iron

do not bleach

drying

stockists

AUSTRALIA:
Australian Country Spinners, Pty Ltd, Level 7, 409 St. Kilda Road, Melbourne Vic 3004.
Tel: 03 9380 3888   Fax: 03 9820 0989   Email: customerservice@auspinners.com.au

AUSTRIA:
Coats Harlander Ges.m.b.H., Autokaderstraße 29, 1210 Wien, Austria
Tel: 00800 26 27 28 00   Fax: (00) 49 7644 802-133 Email: coats.harlander@coats.com
Web: www.coatscrafts.at

BELGIUM:
Coats N.V., c/o Coats GmbH Kaiserstr.1 79341 Kenzingen Germany
Tel: 0032 (0) 800 77 89 2 Fax:00 49 7644 802 133 Email: sales.coatsninove@coats.com
Web: www.coatscrafts.be

BULGARIA:
Coats Bulgaria, 7 Magnaurska Shkola Str., BG-1784 Sofia, Bulgaria
Tel: (+359 2) 976 77 41   Fax: (+359 2) 976 77 20   Email: officebg@coats.com
Web: www.coatsbulgaria.bg

CANADA:
Westminster Fibers, 10 Roybridge Gate, Suite 200, Vaughan, Ontario L4H 3M8
Tel: (800) 263-2354   Fax: 905-856-6184   Email: info@westminsterfibers.com

CHINA:
Coats Shanghai Ltd, No 9 Building , Baosheng Road, Songjiang Industrial Zone, Shanghai.
Tel: (86- 21) 13816681825   Fax: (86-21) 57743733-326   Email: victor.li@coats.com

CYPRUS:
Coats Bulgaria, 7 Magnaurska Shkola Str., BG-1784 Sofia, Bulgaria
Tel: (+359 2) 976 77 41   Fax: (+359 2) 976 77 20   Email: officebg@coats.com
Web: www.coatscrafts.com.cy

CZECH REPUBLIC:
Coats Czecho s.r.o.Staré Mesto 246 569 32
Tel: (420) 461616633   Email: galanterie@coats.com

ESTONIA:
Coats Eesti AS, Ampri tee 9/4, 74001 Viimsi Harjumaa
Tel: +372 630 6250   Fax: +372 630 6260   Email: info@coats.ee   Web: www.coatscrafts.co.ee

DENMARK:
Carl J. Permin A/S Egegaardsvej 28 DK-2610 Rødovre
Tel: (45) 36 72 12 00 E-mail: permin@permin.dk

FINLAND:
Coats Opti Crafts Oy, Huhtimontie 6 04200 KERAVA
Tel: (358) 9 274871Email: coatsopti.sales@coats.com   www.coatscrafts.fi

FRANCE:
Coats France, c/o Coats GmbH, Kaiserstr.1, 79341 Kenzingen, Germany
Tel: (0) 0810 06 00 02   Email: artsdufil@coats.com Web: www.coatscrafts.fr

GERMANY:
Coats GmbH, Kaiserstr. 1, 79341 Kenzingen, Germany
Tel: 0049 7644 802 222   Email: kenzingen.vertrieb@coats.com Fax: 0049 7644 802 300
Web: www.coatsgmbh.de

GREECE:
Coats Bulgaria, 7 Magnaurska Shkola Str., BG-1784 Sofia, Bulgaria
Tel: (+359 2) 976 77 41   Fax: (+359 2) 976 77 20   Email: officebg@coats.com
Web: www.coatscrafts.gr

HOLLAND: Coats B.V., c/o Coats GmbH, Kaiserstr.1, 79341 Kenzingen, Germany
Tel: 0031 (0) 800 02 26 6488 Fax: 00 49 7644 802 133 Email: sales.coatsninove@coats.com
Web: www.coatscrafts.be

HONG KONG:
East Unity Company Ltd, Unit B2, 7/F., Block B, Kailey Industrial Centre, 12 Fung Yip Street, Chai Wan
Tel: (852)2869 7110   Email: eastunityco@yahoo.com.hk

ICELAND:
Storkurinn, Laugavegi 59, 101 Reykjavik
Tel: (354) 551 8258   Email: storkurinn@simnet.is

ITALY:
Coats Cucirini srl, Viale Sarca no 223, 20126 Milano
Tel: 02636151   Fax: 0266111701

KOREA:
Coats Korea Co. Ltd, 5F Eyeon B/D, 935-40 Bangbae-Dong, 137-060
Tel: (82) 2 521 6262   Fax: (82) 2 521 5181   Email: rozenpark@coats.com

LATVIA:
Coats Latvija SIA, Mukusalas str. 41 b, Riga LV-1004
Tel: +371 67 625173   Fax: +371 67 892758   Email: info.latvia@coats.com
Web: www.coatscrafts.lv

LEBANON:
y.knot, Saifi Village, Mkhalissiya Street 162, Beirut
Tel: (961) 1 992211   Fax: (961) 1 315553   Email: y.knot@cyberia.net.lb

LITHUANIA & RUSSIA:
Coats Lietuva UAB, A. Juozapaviciaus str. 6/2, LT-09310 Vilnius
Tel: +370 527 30971   Fax: +370 527 2305   Email: info@coats.lt   Web: www.coatscrafts.lt

LUXEMBOURG:
Coats N.V., c/o Coats GmbH, Kaiserstr.1, 79341 Kenzingen, Germany
Tel: 00 49 7644 802 222   Fax: 00 49 7644 802 133   Email: sales.coatsninove@coats.com
Web: www.coatscrafts.be

MALTA:
John Gregory Ltd, 8 Ta'Xbiex Sea Front, Msida MSD 1512, Malta
Tel: +356 2133 0202   Fax: +356 2134 4745   Email: raygreg@onvol.net

MEXICO:
Estambres Crochet SA de CV, Aaron Saenz 1891-7, PO Box SANTAMARIA, 64650 MONTERREY
TEL +52 (81) 8335-3870

NEW ZEALAND:
ACS New Zealand, P.O Box 76199, Northwood, Christchurch New Zealand
Tel: 64 3 323 6665Fax: 64 3 323 6660 Email: lynn@impactmg.co.nz

NORWAY:
Carl J. Permin A/S Egegaardsvej 28 DK-2610 Rødovre
Tel: (45) 36 72 12 00 E-mail: permin@permin.dk

PORTUGAL:
Coats & Clark, Quinta de Cravel, Apartado 444, 4431-968 Portugal
Tel: 00 351 223 770700

SINGAPORE:
Golden Dragon Store, 101 Upper Cross Street #02-51, People's Park Centre, Singapore 058357
Tel: (65) 6 5358454   Fax: (65) 6 2216278   Email: gdscraft@hotmail.com

SLOVAKIA:
Coats s.r.o.Kopcianska 94851 01 Bratislava
Tel: (421) 263532314   Email: galanteria@coats.com

SOUTH AFRICA:
Arthur Bales LTD, 62 4th Avenue, Linden 2195
Tel: (27) 11 888 2401   Fax: (27) 11 782 6137   Email: arthurb@new.co.za

SPAIN:
Coats Fabra SAU, Avda Meridiana 350, pta 13, 08027 Barcelona
Tel: (34) 932908400   Fax: 932908409   Email: atencion.clientes@coats.com

SWEDEN:
Carl J. Permin A/S Egegaardsvej 28 DK-2610 Rødovre
Tel: (45) 36 72 12 00 E-mail: permin@permin.dk

SWITZERLAND:
Coats Stroppel AG, Stroppelstrasse 20, 5417 Untersiggenthal, Switzerland
Tel: 00800 2627 2800   Fax: 0049 7644 802 133 Email: coats.stroppel@coats.com
Web: www.coatscrafts.ch

TAIWAN:
Cactus Quality Co Ltd, 7FL-2, No. 140, Sec.2 Roosevelt Rd, Taipei, 10084 Taiwan, R.O.C.
Tel: 00886-2-23656527   Fax: 886-2-23656503   Email: cqcl@ms17.hinet.net

THAILAND:
Global Wide Trading, 10 Lad Prao Soi 88, Bangkok 10310
Tel: 00 662 933 9019   Fax: 00 662 933 9110   Email: global.wide@yahoo.com

U.S.A.:
Westminster Fibers, 8 Shelter Drive, Greer, South Carolina, 29650
Tel: (800) 445-9276   Fax: 864-879-9432   Email: info@westminsterfibers.com

U.K: Rowan, Green Lane Mill, Holmfirth, West Yorkshire, England HD9 2DX
Tel: +44 (0) 1484 681881   Fax: +44 (0) 1484 687920   Email: ccuk.sales@coats.com
Web: www.knitrowan.com

rockette

bergen

union

main image page 28 / pattern page 59

main image page 26 / pattern page 47

main image page 16 / pattern page 53

astoria

bellerose

main image page 21 & 4 / pattern page 42

main image page 24 & 18 / pattern page 44

Corona

driscoll

main image page 30 & 10 / pattern page 50

main image page 8 & 13 / pattern page 54

skyland

haven

main image page 36 & 32 / pattern page 61

main image page 38 & 34 / pattern page 56

First published in Great Britain 2015 by Sarah Hatton
www.sarah.hatton.com

Printed in the UK by Lion FPG